CW00855057

SAUCE

THE POETRY VIRGINS
SAUCE

EDITED BY LINDA FRANCE
FOREWORD BY U.A. FANTHORPE

BLOODAXE BOOKS
DIAMOND TWIG PRESS

ISBN: 1 85224 316 3

First published 1994 by
Bloodaxe Books Ltd,
P.O. Box 1SN,
Newcastle upon Tyne NE99 1SN,
in association with
Diamond Twig Press,
5 Bentinck Road,
Newcastle upon Tyne NE4 6UT.

Bloodaxe Books Ltd and Diamond Twig Press
acknowledge the financial assistance of Northern Arts.

Cover printing by J. Thomson Colour Printers Ltd, Glasgow.

Printed in Great Britain by
Bell & Bain Limited, Glasgow, Scotland.

For all our mothers

ACKNOWLEDGEMENTS

Thanks are due to the following for permission to publish the poems in this anthology:

WENDY COPE: To author and Faber & Faber Ltd for 'Reading Scheme' from *Making Cocoa for Kingsley Amis* (1986) and 'A Green Song' from *Serious Concerns* (1992): © Wendy Cope 1986, 1992.

JULIA DARLING: To author for 'Small Beauties' from *Small Beauties* (Newcastle Libraries, 1988) and 'Buying Cars' and 'Forecasting' from *Modern Goddess* (Diamond Twig Press, 1992).

MARIA JASTRZEBSKA: To author for 'Which of Us Wears the Trousers', published by Virago Press in *Naming the Waves* (1988): © Maria Jastrzebska 1988.

ELMA MITCHELL: To author and Peterloo Poets for 'Thoughts After Ruskin' from *People Etc: Poems New & Selected* (1987): © Elma Mitchell 1987.

ELLEN PHETHEAN: To author for 'Mine', first published in *Iron Erotica* (Iron Press, 1994), and for 'Mushy Peas', first published in *First Time*.

ANNA SWIR: To Margaret Marshment for 'Her Belly' from *Fat Like the Sun* by Anna Swir, translated by Margaret Marshment and Grazyna Baran (Women's Press, 1986): © Margaret Marshment 1986.

Thanks are also due to the following who helped with this book: June Portlock, a one-time Virgin; Ursula Fanthorpe for her enthusiastic support; Linda France for her care and sympathetic editing; Nicki Taylor for her photographs; Christine Tomkins of Westgate Hill School; Scobie and McIntosh for the loan of the *Sauce* outfits; Bev Robinson; *The Crack*; Jenny Attala, Kitty Fitzgerald and Chrissie Glazebrook at Northern Arts; and Karin Young for her photocopier.

CONTENTS

FOREWORD

Readers have got used to women novelists, who have been around since Fanny Burney. But women poets tend to be regarded dubiously as something new, which probably began in that suspect era, the Sixties. This is quite wrong. Women poets go back at least to Sappho, who was such a brilliant writer that the Church Fathers burnt almost all of her work.

The women writers whose work appears in this anthology are bright too, and no doubt if there were Church Fathers around still the fires would still be burning. They write poems about the things men don't notice, or don't bother with: about bras, moles, trousers, and the smell men leave in bathrooms; about things women wear, or mend, or clean up. But this is not domesticated poetry because it is about hoovers. Poetry is liberation, and these are the women who got away, who are redefining themselves with a new accuracy, who write, like Anna Swir, about having a fat belly because she's had five children, or about which of two lesbians wears the trousers, or about making a bechamel sauce. They write with economy and wit; they write with feeling and justice; they write with accuracy and pain; and above all they write out of love.

All poetry is about love, or anger, which is love reversed. What women poets are doing is extending the range of things and people that can be loved.

U.A. FANTHORPE

PREFACE

The only coy thing about the Poetry Virgins is their name, which arose from the fact that when they first started giving performances in the North East seven years ago, they were all new to the game. As were many of their audiences: they have played at Trades Union conferences, Women's Health courses, rallies, pubs, cabarets and colleges as well as the more traditional arts venues. They may have been virgins once but now they have become real professionals, inviting us to share their shameless delight in how The First Time should always be – vital, authentic, passionate, hilarious.

Sauce represents the cream of their recent work, with the odd soupçon from an earlier anthology, *Modern Goddess* (Diamond Twig, 1992). Most of the poems in the book are written by Julia Darling and Ellen Phethean, with contributions by other women writers, both new and established. Julia and Ellen form part of the Poetry Virgins line-up, alongside Charlie Hardwick, Kay Hepplewhite and Fiona MacPherson, an exciting chemistry of acting and writing skills.

The poems on the page, as well as in performance, are marked by an unusual fearlessness and refreshing positive humour. These are women not afraid to open their big mouths, break taboos, stand up and be wise *and* foolish. They are provocative and challenging, imaginative and entertaining. Their spirit is one of celebration and co-operation.

An evening with the Poetry Virgins is one of initiation, hilarity and mayhem. Their appetites are boundless. There are poems about bodies and bras, childhood and cars, sex, sport and drinking. They sing out loud and clear in the broad and strong register of a woman's voice. Like all virgins, they are too good for this world. But they're also bad and brave enough to change that world by breaking the silence and stirring the sauce.

If you're reading this after seeing the Poetry Virgins live and kicking, you'll already have a taste for it. If you haven't, treat your-self and try some of their *Sauce*.

LINDA FRANCE

Journey with a Golden Lady

I want to touch
the golden lady
who has stood too long
alone and cold
above the jewellers

I want to climb with her
up onto the chimneys

in the highest arches
of this bandy city
I will kiss her

like cherubs do

our hearts will hang
like starlings from the ledges

we will step amongst
the chiselled world
of brickies' experiments

stroke the gargoyles
that no one ever sees

climbing the lofty lofts
of an ultimate arch

on our way to heaven
halfway anyway

spiralling
up

JULIA DARLING

Ancestry

Have you ever seen my extraordinary feet?
They are waders, descended from flippers.
My little toe is related to a prehistoric mollusc.

My legs are Gothic pillars designed in Barnet
by Presbyterians, who sang *Jerusalem*.
These columns could support cathedrals.

My womb is a wartime nurse,
functional, regular, robust.
A womb that purses its lips.

My belly is the pillow that old ladies die on.
It's Victorian linen, the best in the high street.
It clasps my insides with invisible darns.

My breasts are Scottish, from a line of sepia aunts,
who wrapped their Bristols tightly in sealy cloths,
with nipples as distant as Iona.

Unfortunately my shoulders are related
to sorry uncles, they hunch and apologise,
sag and wait sadly for sympathetic arms.

But these fine ears are sisters of the sails
that carried cargoes off the flat sea.
They are adventurous and foolhardy.

And this face, that berates me at the hairdresser
and winces in bar mirrors is mine.
I moulded it from ancestral clay.

All mine, with its thumb prints
and crevices. It's not finished
You can have it when I'm done.

JULIA DARLING

Turkish Bath

can I suggest
we take our towels
down to those curtained rooms
beneath the municipal
city baths

where the blue water
slops heavy above
in bright chlorine blue
but down there it's ochre
snug and frowsty
as blankets

your skin can safely
open all its pores
we will take off our rings
and belts and buckles
and lie in those small
velvet rooms for ladies
who like to rest
in the afternoon

pink and pummiced
we can be quiet as eggs
together in that steamy
labyrinth

like courtesans
waiting, dreaming
and awake

bare feet in the corridors
gossip of intimates
soft wet marble

salt lick

JULIA DARLING

Nesting

She envied the freedom of birds:
skylarks rising in the spring sun,
banter of glossy blackbirds,
swifts and swallows
singing migratory
transatlantic epics,
redbreasted robins dabbing toes
in forbidden snowy gardens;
even a scabby pigeon
slumming it on a high town ledge
seemed luckier than she was.

Her moving dreams
of treetops and wind-riding thermals
grounded by the flightless path.
Until that once-in-a-lifetime day:
left alone at the altar,
white net flapping,
screaming like a gull fleeing stormy seas,
she flew away.

Meticulously, twig by leaf,
a bird's eye for detail,
she built her branchy home.
People whispered.
She simply smiled and whistled.
Her parents, mortified, visited once, left mystified.

Neighbours brought her necessities, and, later,
her pension; she so rarely spoke
her voice croaked, scaring the paper boy.

After fifty years of tree-living,
they found her sparrow bones,
flute-clean, foetal in her nest,
and brought her down to earth
at last.

ELLEN PHETHEAN

Taking Flight

She always knew she would grow wings
and had mentioned her tingling shoulder blades

to the adults, red and portly in the sitting-room
who chuckled at the joke and shut the door.

As a young woman she made an earth
in her room and learnt not to talk of them aloud.

But sometimes at night she woke
hearing feathers rustling under skin.

People said, perhaps she needs therapy.
She's tense and shifty round the neck.

And she tried everything, until she saw
there was no cure (Immac stung the tips).

I'm not like other girls, she wailed.
It's hellish in this wingless world.

Grounded, hoping some sweet eye
would sense her secret, stroke her growing span.

A woman now, frozen in her shoes,
wiping kitchens, shopping, drinking gin.

Until one night she looks above the trees,
hears whispering and jollity up there,

squints to see winged women soaring by
with confidence and smiles as cool as glass.

She lost her job, her wings didn't fit in.
She's poor, but saves on busfares, watches out

for girls down on the street in anoraks
who hang their heads and wish they had no wings.

JULIA DARLING

Newcastle Is Lesbos

Sweating in the Turkish baths
or breast stroking in Elswick pool.
Driving buses, besuited, unrooted,
or regularly walking The Barking Dog.

Browsing in the bookshop.
Camping with Vamps in twilight,
rocking with Doris afterwards.
Teaming into the Tyneside.

Plotting on allotments on Sundays.
Playing footsie in the park,
on television, on telephones.
Flirting in Fenwicks.

Newcastle is Lesbos.
They have infiltrated. Look behind you,
under your desk, in the garden,
in your pink rose bushes.

Sappho, come here on holiday instead.
We are in commune with our own Powerhouse.
Come, give praises to our Northern ladies.

The Heat is On.
There's Spit on our Tongues.
We're best in the West,
Walker or Byker
or cruising the wide waters
of the Tyne.

Remember that nice doctor,
social worker, dentist (dammit)
and the woman who winked at you
by the pyjamas in Marks and Spencers?

Newcastle is Lesbos.
They seem quite ordinary,
they are quite ordinary.
We are.

JULIA DARLING

My Mother Said

Bames, Buntysweet,
Bonks and A-Becket,
naming her brood
like a farmer's wife.
Momo, wetty, winkle – words
safe as blancmange
bosoms in opaque nighties.
Maresy doats and
the blush fucket,
don't step in the
dogsh.
Reaching for blankets,
words surface,
spoonerish and nursery-rude
out of my mouth, her rubbish talk
that smooths, soothes
difficult little lives.

ELLEN PHETHEAN

Poetry Is Fashion

Poems will be short this year.
The adaptable haiku
can be a sparkling seventeen syllables
of silver lamé or a sombre three lines
of grey and charcoal.

Poets will be worn out this season,
wowing them from Halifax to Hackney,
reading, writing, stirring
the excitement with their
launches of fabulous new collections

New poetry, with a natural look,
aggressively-now verse
and careful cut of rhythms,
has sent a frisson
through the High Street names.

A slim volume is the 'in' accessory,
nestling in jacket pocket
or swung casually
in the hand.
Check out the new generation
of word designers.

ELLEN PHETHEAN

Buying a Brassière

My mother told me self-esteem
is rooted in a well-built brassière.
After that a girl should
prioritise her feet.
So I'm standing breast-naked
with Sheila from Lingerie.
She rubs her cool hands
to warm them and wields
a tape measure around my secret skins.
Do you know what I think?
I think in all her smooth experience
she has never seen knockers
as weird as these.
Luminous from darkness,
puckered as jellyfish.
Unrelated spaniels' ears.

She piles up boxes
of hoists and straps
designed by welders
and by lunchtime
we have excavated
a brassière, which I call
Cleopatra, because it is heroic
with enormous bowls
of fragile lace, and hooks
with black splendid eyes.

Sheila writes the size on tissue paper
for posterity, glad to see
my flat back.

I bool off. Well hung, separated.
And the world is different now.
Even men on building sites
are silenced, in awe
of my magnificent frontage.

JULIA DARLING

Picassoesque

once I reviled
these stout ankles

ungraceful fetlocks
thick as lamp posts

I even strapped them
into sadistic tight
black leather boots
squeezed them until
they went blue with height

then she told me
one blousy afternoon

naked on a town roof
that they were picassoesque

picassoesque

and I fell in love
spent nights with art books
looking for ankles

shoeless, with wide
painted legs above

so look down
to your sturdiest joints
turn away from
insignificant ankles
in glossy magazines

and you too could be vogueish
in your wide and beautiful curves

JULIA DARLING

Good Taste

She wants to wear a torn netting skirt,
a creased and glittering rag
and a plastic flower in her hair.

Just a flower, she cries, *and lipstick*
And my angel shoes!

It's raining, I say, with bad faith.
When you're wet
and your ankles shiver
above insubstantial socks
your flower will droop
and you won't thank me.

But I know
in that other world
there is no cold.
Only the warmth
of other girls' shoes.

All she desires
on a grey January morning
is a bit of glitz,
the stuff that Barbi's made of,
something to flounce.

I catch her tears.
You are beautiful
without all this paraphernalia.
But she has slipped off,
stolen lipstick in her pocket,
corned beef legs
against the freezing winds,

head aflame with visions of elegance,
dreams of good taste.

JULIA DARLING

Moles

like the moles on my face
rough skin of my hands
weak flesh of my belly
red stains in my eyes

the scars on my knees
the crease on my neck
nicotine on my teeth
and cracks in my lips

I am not renewable
I will never wear pearls
I won't fold my arms
and wait in the playground

you can blush and despair
wish for a crisp, brisk parent
wish for fairy cakes
and tupperware

but I am indelible
unlike you, unmarked
changeable
and I made you

JULIA DARLING

Small Beauties

Let the milk boil over;
the half-filled tins of baked beans sit on the table,
children scribble on the walls with crayons,
clothes heap in riotous mountains.

I am reading a book.

Let the bells ring, bills lie unopened,
doors slam open then bash shut, letters unwritten,
plants unwatered, bread get hard as a rock.

I am thinking about the moon.

Let the bank get nasty, the grass grow high,
children decorate themselves with lipstick,
build houses within houses in every room,
pee on the floor, pull dolls' heads off.

I am looking for a door.

Oh, come here, you small beauties,
together we shall run across the town moor,
with waving fingers, running for our lives.

You are too small, and too beautiful, to ignore.

JULIA DARLING

Playing Pool

We all know
what we're talking about.

The silver is on the table.
The triangle of coloured spheres
will break.

Me or him.
He'll never live it down
if I win.

That's why I'm ambitious and hot
wanting to beat him
black, purple and blue,
playing pool like a boy
with my eyes down
in the low shabby spotlight
of a yellow room.

Me or him.

The male chorus
gurgling on Guinness
hangs from the ceiling.

Balls roll, like the eyes
peering at my arse
as I bend and squint,
arch over backwards
with professional
amateur dramatics.

And pocket mouths
close and twist
as we click on
desperately.

Me or him.

The last ball hangs like smoke,
snookered, caught in its blind trap.

And how they love me when I lose.
They love me when I lose.

JULIA DARLING

World Cup Summer

Gawky. Eight. She stares
at a fright of magpie strips
flapping towards her.

Come on LADS!

thunders coach,
a man whose tea is now baking.
She shrugs, attempting indifference,
lopes to his whistle.

Come ON lads!
Pace. PACE.
Tuck in behind him.
Worry him.

Coach is FIFA, I am Big Jack,
agitated beyond the white line,
longing to run to her
with water.

DON'T JUST STAND THERE, TACKLE!

If football is theatre,
don't let my girl be an understudy.
Coach doesn't hear.
He has made her a sub,
practising skills on the sideline,

and at night she will paste
footballers' shaven faces
into her scrapbook,
dreaming of shinpads.

Oh god of football and improbability,
let Ireland win the World Cup.

And let her keep a foothold
On this uneven pitch.

JULIA DARLING

Early Morning Swim

Sometimes, gliding smoothly along the slow lane
we touch, and recoil in shock
as this is a solitary and private affair
though we know each others' bodies so well.

Watching each other with covert glances
in familiar rituals of dressing, undressing,
each mole and scar, sagging breasts, scrawny arms
are recognised like old friends
by the sisterhood who meet silently
each morning.

There are men, certainly, young blades
with hairy chests, tattoos, mouths grimacing
splashing violently down the fast lane.

We women are different,
stately as swans we glide
up and down, up and down,
arms circling, pushing away encumbrances.

VICKY DARLING

Mine

Dark vulva, sucking ridged muscle,
flame-streaked power,
contracting rhythmically,
swallowing men fruitfully
down to the sump.

Orange flushed, she expands
to accommodate fingers, tools
working at the seam belt,
mucously hot and wet,
lubricating the movement.

Then, airless and gripping,
cavernously claustrophobic,
she squeezes dry, draining
to physical exhaustion
those blackened diggers,
grey-hued, ill-lit, feeling the route;

mouthing 'enough', suddenly
she clamps tight, closing her jaws,
eating or spewing,
secretly dangerous,
the hot body interior.

ELLEN PHETHEAN

Coming Out

1

that difficult
morass
the silence
before
saying it

when birds fly
round your heart
and the sound
of kettles boiling
is unnaturally
loud

and you skirt
around the kitchen

making odd noises
like words

knowing
that what you want
to say
is both unnecessary
and vital

so that
when you say it

if you say it

you grow wings
and smile
with both the corners
of your mouth

2

after I said it
there was a quietness

a bereavement

a sullen holding back of hands

you said

ah well, shall we go to Bainbridges then?

I said

perhaps flowers would be in order

but you were dwelling
on difficult aunts
who had the sense
to be spinsters

three years on
I still hang on your words

ask me how she is
ask me if we're well

do you know we still
sleep in the same bed?

and what I said in 1991
still holds, was not a phase?

my ex-husband is fine I think
I saw him yesterday

for coffee and yes
we're as friendly as ever

but she is the flame
that won't go out

Ask me how she is
Ask me if we're well

JULIA DARLING

Which of Us Wears the Trousers

Behind the liberal politeness
You're dying to know
Instead of the chat about societal attitudes
What you'd really like to ask is
Which of us in this relationship
Wears the trousers.

I'll tell you
Since you want to know so much
And since it's really very simple:
I do
And then again
She does
And then sometimes
Neither of us
Wears any trousers at all.

MARIA JASTRZEBSKA

Men Like Her Father

have voluminous voices,
swallow whole rooms
with their overtones.

Restaurants shrink
in the benign bigness
of their mouths.

Cathedral-wide hands
clap and shake,
awkwardly search
the glove compartments
of cars.

Ahoy there, through the trumpets
of palms.

Other people
must seem like twigs, paper
to such oversize men,

with real braces, garters,
great trouser buttons
shirts of stiff linen,

who leave a pungent gamey scent
in the bathroom

and sit in armchairs
with heavy books from bookclubs
on Cromwell and Napoleon

reading aloud, with windy
irritated voices,

for those too reckless to hear,
for those who can't tie knots,
for those who leave the tops off bottles.

JULIA DARLING

Be Kind

Be kind to white male southern students
who in post-acne anxiousness lumber
down the narrow pedestrian walkway
on their way to slowly open bank accounts.

Be tolerant. Even though they keep
meeting each other, neighing like donkeys,
swinging their half-cut hair and strappy bags,
standing in heavy clumps.

Don't think about their parents in Surrey,
or blame them for bending
your windscreen wipers, or roaring rude words
when even the birds sleep.

Or shudder at their purchases in corner shops,
Pot Noodles, Fray Bentos, Vesta and peas.
Or imagine their corner of a communal fridge,
their lonely anglepoises, their non-stick milk pans.

Perhaps they are homesick, worrying about
their parents' divorces, and yesterday's essay.
Or have agonising lovebites on tender shoulders.
Or are wishing they had gone to Exeter, or Bath.

So don't attack them on your bicycle,
grazing their shins as you pass,
not saying sorry.

They don't all vote Conservative
and pull their trousers down.

JULIA DARLING

Geronimo!

Geronimo...!
You and I'd go
jumping off
the high ledge
into the sandy pool.
We'd shout
as we launched
into airy gravity:
Fat Bum, Brillo Pad, Clive is a ...
Once
a secret slipped
I Love You
into that waterfall
of bodies and words.
Your face caught it
mid-smile
before the splash.
But like the emperor's
new clothes
we never
ever mentioned it.

ELLEN PHETHEAN

Mr Right

Are ye courtin yet, pet?
No? Lookin for Mr Right?
Mr Right'll come along, divvint fret,
but you're not even courtin yet!

Our Peggy's engaged, did I tell ye?
She was seventeen, so they thought why not?
How old are ye? Nineteen!
Nineteen, lookin for Mr Right.
Well, don't be too fussy, will ye!

Our Mary's been married since she was sixteen.
She's got two bairns right now. And you're not
even courtin. Lookin for Mr Right!
Well ye'll not find him in a book, that's for sure.

Ye want to get married soon, pet.
Ye want to get your bairns settled
before ye're too old – right?
Get on with it!

Ye'll have to get yersel to the dance, man.
Ye'll soon find yersel a lad. But mind,
if ye wait for Mr Right,
ye'll never get started courtin!

JUNE P. PORTLOCK

Forecasting

He was a viking in his forties.
Tyne after tyne I said, don't dogger me,
just don't dogger me – but he fishered,
me a single parent with no german bite.

I came to like his humber,
and eventually thames towards him.
Dover and dover
we caught the white of each others lundy,
throwing all faeroes into the fast net,
deep in our irish sea,
rockallin' and dancin' the mallin.
Those were the hebrides years.
Until Cromarty.

How I wish Cromarty had not met my viking.

Still only forty, we tyned and doggered,
until my fisher ran out.
And he got his german bite all right,
humbering halfway up the Thames,
waves dover him,
his white in the dark lundy,
faeroes swept from the fast net.

I have drunk the Irish Sea,
hearing him, calling through ships,

Rockall – Mallin – CROMARTY!

Thanks Cromarty. I hope you sink,
someday.

JULIA DARLING

Cranes

Blue and yellow cranes necking on the bank,
tall irises of the dry dock
stippled with rust,
kiss goodbye
under a mackerel sky.

ELLEN PHETHEAN

Brockenhurst Station

While changing trains at Brockenhurst
a woman starts screaming.

The long platform trembles with her
wild octaves. Newspapers flutter
with her hurricane breaths.

British Rail acts slowly.
An official stands morose
in a dusty jacket before her.

He pushes down her decibels
with his hands.
British silence hangs
amongst us.

We get nervous.
She screams like our babies
at night. We single
into islands.

And the train heaves in
like an old saviour,
dragging open its doors
shielding us from her blast.

I am pulled away,
sandwiched between
large men reading
small novels.

Safe. I think.

JULIA DARLING

Sky

I bought a piece of sky.
It's mine, I said,
that bit over there,
enough blue to patch
a sailor's trousers.
But a man said
No, he owned that bit
and a lot more.
When I looked again
I wasn't sure.
Then a French company
leased clouds
that covered my little patch
of blue,
said they owned the rain
that fell.
So what the hell,
I can still look.
But a recently privatised sun
only shines intermittently now
and many nations
are in a legal wrangle
over the shares of
night and day.
A solicitor said
my contract
was worthless.

At night I dream
of cirrus clouds,
morning stars
and blue reflections.

ELLEN PHETHEAN

A Green Song

to sing at the bottle-bank

One green bottle,
Drop it in the bank.
Ten green bottles,
What a lot we drank.
Heaps of bottles
And yesterday's a blank
But we'll save the planet,
Tinkle, tinkle, clank!

We've got bottles –
Nice, percussive trash.
Bags of bottles
Cleaned us out of cash.
Empty bottles,
We love to hear them smash
And we'll save the planet,
Tinkle, tinkle, crash!

WENDY COPE

The Old Country

They might dress me in pink
and enable me. A stout girl
in slacks will hold my hand
and sway to inconceivable music.
I will smile, like an old tiger
and stamp my feet; look beyond
her great liquid eyes to the country
they will not let me lie in.

Or some bearded bloke on placement
will nod gravely at my dim rememberings
and type it up. My lies could become
posters on buses, or be published
in a bright paperback that I never see.
Afterwards I would wonder where
he was, that visitor with his biro.

That secret country of senility,
still uncharted, dangerous, edgeless.
Who will fashion my old age?
Will my children write letters
about me that I never read?
Will I remember to reminisce
and paint primitive flowers?
Or be a ghoul whose raging hands
and feet only appear to dance.

JULIA DARLING

Cherry Trees Nursing Home

I'm not going to stop asking.
My body's tired of me,
gypsies dance on my curtains at night.
I couldn't get there in time.
I said Give me a mop and bucket,
I'll do it.
A woman rocks a baby, wanders round my room.
That Marjorie, sits next to me,
talks, it's no good
I can't hear a word.
I'm not afraid of dying if that's what you think.
This isn't my sort of place,
not my kind of people.
I ignore them.
Sunlight splashes my walls, leaves beckon.
I used to watch *Dynasty*.
Nice clothes, no use here.
I can't read anymore.
It's a lot of fantossle.
I belong Lobley Hill.
The ocean rolls through my room.

What have I done wrong
that you haven't taken me?
I miss my bungalow
and Smudgie by the fire.
I weep, I can't help myself.
Edna didn't come.
Well, only for two minutes.
She just lives round the corner!
I hear singing.
You've forgotten me, God.
Some of the girls are friendly
but they take my money.
I haven't left it on the dresser.

Mother brushes my hair, ties my ribbon.
Can we go for a walk?
Mother, take me?

ELLEN PHETHEAN

Her Belly

She has a right to have a fat belly,
her belly has borne five children.
They warmed themselves at it,
it was the sun of their childhood.

The five children have gone,
her fat belly remains.
This belly
is beautiful.

ANNA SWIR
translated by Margaret Marshment & Grazyna Baran

Surfing

Recklessly she plunges in
swims out to meet the tidal wave

sick with excitement
she strains to crest the monster
before it topples
crashing her beneath

each wave comes on inexorably
will she ride it
or be ridden into the ground
round and round rasped onto the gritty floor

she treads water
gently floating breathing easy
as she watches the next giant
approaching

detached and calm she can ride them
easy so big and powerful
lifted over the top
if she stays in control

if she mistimes the rhythm or panics
muscles tired with swimming
she'll drown she knows

ELLEN PHETHEAN

Mushy Peas

There isn't room in my crowded body
for a baby and poetry. Creative clashes
leave me blank.
Little feet kick out the ideas,
reveries punched away by active fists.

Snacks creep into my villanelles,
orange juice floods my rhyming.
I am diverted
like a new-dug canal on a sandy beach
by someone else's whim.

Blank pages fill me with longings
to sleep dreamlessly, hijacked
to a different airport
on awakening.

My brain sogs to mushy peas.
But like a compost heap
deep inside the process is hotting up.
Next year I will be fertile again.

ELLEN PHETHEAN

Young Male Poet

He asked for a mirror
from the audience.

In silence he regarded himself.
As did the audience.

Then he shouted at himself.
And the audience.

Got feedback from his mike
but not the audience.

ELLEN PHETHEAN

Men on Trains 1

The man next to me has a suit on
and a vaguely balding head.
He studies a paper on microchips
And his suit is so pressed it's dead.

But every half an hour or so
he roots through his executive case
and brings out a vial of perfume
that he dabs on his wrist and his face.

Men on Trains 2

The big man who sits opposite
Is holding a mobile phone.
He dials a number carefully
And listens to it drone.

Someone answers and he says
Hallo hallo it's me.
His voice is oddly dangerous.
I pretend to drink cold tea.

I'm phoning from the hospital
He whines. (We shunt past Leeds).
*The operation might not work
Or perhaps they can cure me.*

Perhaps they can cure me,
He says, while nibbling a bit of cheese,
*I just wish you'd phone me up
sometimes. Just once. Please.*

JULIA DARLING

48

Men on Trains 3

Too large for 125s,
his trousers fill
two seats, though
one is mine.
I sigh and rearrange
the baby on my lap.
Too long for British Rail size,
his crossed legs
wrap mine
under the table.
Unhappy feet kick
my Tesco bag.
His head dips and bends
searching for them,
apologising for his
unruly impediments.
Too single for a Family
Rail Card, his briefcase,
coat and clipboard
hog the table,
displacing bricks, drinks
and nappy sacks.
He smiles
sympathetically
at my disarray.
I smile back.
Both of us outlaws
in the Nottingham Forest
of Charters
for standard customers.

ELLEN PHETHEAN

Design Fault

YOU MUST PRESS THE LOCK BUTTON
or this is what could happen:
The doors will open slowly
and it takes hours to shut them.

I recall those pleasant doors
on trains with broken locks.
You could hold them closed manually,
apologise to knocks.

Now a carriageful of businessmen
on the express train to Leeds
has seen me gaping helplessly
above my naked knees.

JULIA DARLING

Below the Boot

I lost my exhaust
without a backward glance
with aplomb,
like a woman
stepping out of her knickers
when the elastic's gone.
Coolly disregarding
the gratuitous hoots
of men's horns,
showing no interest
in the clatter
from below the boot,
I simply drove on
roaring,
leaving it where it lay.
Making a mental note
to return later
incognito
and collect it.

ELLEN PHETHEAN

Losing My Teeth 1

Rachel has a bust,
moves amongst the mares,
robust and ruddy,
at ease with horse flesh.

I have no bust.
Bones suffocate
between the girths.
Saddled with nausea

I ride my nerves, jumpy
as Sheik, my black pony.
I dare to trot.
He canters to mount

the piebald gypsy mares
loose on the common.
Rachel shouts instructions
Use your knees. Curb him!

Rachel laughs, knows how to
command with her thighs.
I am crying, clinging
to his arching back,

my legs aching for the ground,
the smell of hide in my throat
dragged along for the ride.
This isn't a game.

ELLEN PHETHEAN

Losing My Teeth 2

Deft as a circus performer,
impossible as a cartoon,
in slow motion I fly,
one foot in, one out.

My uneven stirrups betray
my innocence, hopeless
with horses, feeble
with leather belt buckles.

I let go of everything:
reins, mind, hope –
Leave it to Fate,
and my out-of-sight instructor.

Fate meets tussock, eats
grass, bumps along
the common again and again,
one leg restrained,

the other waving foolishly,
like a bad joke.
Film sequence hooves
canter inches from my ear.

The farce reaches its dénouement.
Sheik shakes me off, gallops away,
leaving me with a ballooning leg
and a colourful stir-fry face.

ELLEN PHETHEAN

Fourteen Units

(after watching breakfast television)

Curse you doctor, burn in hell,
and that community nurse as well.
I once believed that you knew best
and tried to curb my grim excess.

Counting units, sad and guilty,
as I gulped to unit thirty,
imagining liverish entropy
as punishment for indulgency.

Then, with serious jubilation
Richard and Judy told the nation
that we may be merry, we may drink
pints before we reach the brink.

So who decided that fourteen
should be the lucky numerine?
Men, that's who it was, I bet,
who fear a drunken female sot.

Who like their tea prepared on time,
not cooked by someone sloshed on wine.
And we all know a proper mother
Is sober as a teapot cover.

JULIA DARLING

Thoughts After Ruskin

Women reminded him of lilies and roses.
Me they remind rather of blood and soap,
Armed with a warm rag, assaulting noses,
Ears, neck, mouth and all the secret places:

Armed with a sharp knife, cutting up liver,
Holding hearts to bleed under a running tap,
Gutting and stuffing, pickling and preserving,
Scalding, blanching, broiling, pulverising,
– All the terrible chemistry of their kitchens.

Their distant husbands lean across mahogany
And delicately manipulate the market,
While safe at home, the tender and the gentle
Are killing tiny mice, dead snap by the neck,
Asphyxiating flies, evicting spiders,
Scrubbing, scouring aloud, disturbing cupboards,
Committing things to dustbins, twisting, wringing,
Wrists red and knuckles white and fingers puckered,
Pulpy, tepid. Steering screaming cleaners
Around the snags of furniture, they straighten
And haul out sheets from under the incontinent
And heavy old, stoop to importunate young,
Tugging, folding, tucking, zipping, buttoning,
Spooning in food, encouraging excretion,
Mopping up vomit, stabbing cloth with needles,
Contorting wool around their knitting needles,
Creating snug and comfy on their needles.

Their huge hands! their everywhere eyes! their voices
Raised to convey across the hullabaloo,
Their massive thighs and breasts dispensing comfort,
Their bloody passages and hairy crannies,
Their wombs that pocket a man upside down!

And when all's over, off with overalls,
Quickly consulting clocks, they go upstairs,
Sit and sigh a little, brushing hair,
And somehow find, in mirrors, colours, odours,
Their essences of lilies and of roses.

ELMA MITCHELL

Recipes for Disaster

1

First, have a bad night, e.g. the baby woke at four, five and six,
then take a smattering of PMT,
bloated breasts, weepiness and snap your head off.
Mix with intransigent children,
any sex or age, the older ones are tougher.
Finally drop in one unsympathetic partner,
and watch the temperature rise.

2

Find a local hospital,
take one closed ward, two or three OAPs
waiting for hip replacements,
a child needing emergency stitching.
Add together with a junior housedoctor,
preferably overworked.
Invite a local Tory politician to speak,
then fry him.

3

You must leave too little time for this recipe.
Go to town in the car,
put a nagging parent and/or child in the back,
run low on petrol and stall,
lose a parking spot to a man
in a BMW.
Time it so that you have three minutes
before the bank closes,
then park on a Loading Bay.
Leave for ten minutes.
When you return you'll have a £30 ticket,
Lovely!

4

Select a scorching Bank Holiday
and about a hundred thousand people,
squash them onto a narrow quayside,
stuff the children with ice cream, and soak the adults with alcohol.
Leave to stew all day,
stir occasionally to avoid burning.
This should reduce to a red hot paste,
perfect for family picnics.

ELLEN PHETHEAN

Reading Scheme

Here is Peter. Here is Jane. They like fun.
Jane has a big doll. Peter has a ball.
Look, Jane, look! Look at the dog! See him run!

Here is Mummy. She has baked a bun.
Here is the milkman. He has come to call.
Here is Peter. Here is Jane. They like fun.

Go Peter! Go Jane! Come, milkman, come!
The milkman likes Mummy. She likes them all.
Look, Jane, look! Look at the dog! See him run!

Here are the curtains. They shut out the sun.
Let us peep! On tiptoe Jane! You are small!
Here is Peter. Here is Jane. They like fun.

I hear a car, Jane. The milkman looks glum.
Here is Daddy in his car. Daddy is tall.
Look, Jane, look! Look at the dog! See him run!

Daddy looks very cross. Has he a gun?
Up milkman! Up milkman! Over the wall!
Here is Peter. Here is Jane. They like fun.
Look, Jane, look! Look at the dog! See him run!

WENDY COPE

Buying Cars

Do not do what I have done,
you'll end up lost on the cold M1
or stranded with your big end gone.
Do not do what I have done.

Don't trust men with MOTs
who offer Fiestas with guarantees,
and never say thank you and never say please
while handing you over the grimy keys

of the shining Fiesta that shudders inside.
It's really a Lada with bits on the side,
a Frankenstein, with its ends untied,
its linings and bearings all tangled and fried.

And when you return with a dying car,
you'll find that Terry has gone to the bar,
and Michael has gone off looking for scrap,
and Gary says... they'll phone you back.

So zip up your jacket, hold up your chin
and unravel the mysteries of the engine within.
Study your manual, don't believe him
when he says he's adjusted your steering pin.

No don't believe Terry or Gary or Pete
who hide in the alleys behind every street.
Join the RAC or use your feet
and buy some spanners... reet!

Just don't do what I have done.
There's nowhere so lonely as the cold M1,
as the hard shoulder with your big end gone.
Do not do what I have done.

JULIA DARLING

Political Correctness

I chased my daughter down the street
because of what she said
in public, in Australia.
I sent her straight to bed.

Ma, she said to my earnest face,
I'm sick of you droning on
about Aboriginal this and that,
the crimes that we have done.

Daughter, I yelled, these are murderous facts.
You must understand what I say.
So what, she said, if we killed the lot?
It's just The English Way.

JULIA DARLING

Birds in the Chimney

In the end
we are all winged birds
caught in chimneys.

Crashing around rooms
searching for doors.

Believing, with our beating hearts
that somewhere in a dark hole

there is light.

A place where our wings
can find their span.
Where safety
is open plan,
boundaries
are all beneath our feet.

We daren't stop flying at the wall
until we drop, exhausted

surrendering to
our pokey rooms.
The confines of
rectangular years.

JULIA DARLING

Sauce

She said *I'm good at sauces, Bechamel is my best,*
let me show you. Chammy leather hands
cradled ivory bone handle,
warmed the gliding blade,
sliced the butter just so, silver cleaving
thick yellow ounces, so pat.
She let it slide, slow lava
into the heavy solid warmth
of a Le Creuset pan, melting gold,
alchemy over a low blue flame.

Before it browned, still sizzling like an oily sun,
she pulled the cork lid of a stone crock,
ladled soft white flour with powdery hands,
stirred it in, easy as snow, with a worn wooden spoon.
Butter and flour, compliant amber sand
clinging to the sides.

She handled the milk bottle deftly,
the cow-creamy liquid measured
drop by drop by eye,
teasing rutted furrows into silky rivers,
with a masseuse touch. Adjusting the flame,
her fingers firm around the wood,
she worked over the heat stirring, stirring,
her wrist action relentless,
beating, timing, thickening
the sauce in the hot pan
until, judging the exact moment,
her pink tongue licked the spoon.
And she smiled, satisfied.

ELLEN PHETHEAN

BIOGRAPHICAL NOTES

Wendy Cope was born in 1945. She is a bestselling poet and children's writer. Her books include two collections from Faber, *Making Cocoa for Kingsley Amis* (1986) and *Serious Concerns* (1992), a collection of finger rhymes for children, *Twiddling Your Thumbs* (Faber, 1988), a collaboration with artist Nicholas Garland, *The River Girl* (Faber, 1991), and an anthology of women's poetry for teenagers, *Is That the New Moon?* (Collins, 1989).

Julia Darling was the first Virgin. Born in 1956, she is a freelance writer, and lives in Newcastle with her daughters Florrie and Scarlet. Her poetry pamphlet *Small Beauties* was published by Newcastle Libraries in 1988. She is currently writing a novel and finishing a book of short stories (to be published by Panurge). Her plays include *Rafferty's Café, Head of Steel* and (in progress) *Black Diamonds* (Quondam Arts Trust), and *Growing Pains* (Tyne Wear Theatre in Education). She won the Tyne Tees *Put It In Writing* short story competition in 1993.

Vicky Darling is currently Warden of Winchester Friends' Meeting House. 'Early Morning Swim' is her first published poem.

U.A. Fanthorpe is a freelance writer, and lives in Gloucestershire. Her *Selected Poems* (Peterloo, 1986) is published in paperback by Penguin, and she has published five other collections with Peterloo, most recently *A Watching Brief* (1987) and *Neck-Verse* (1992).

Linda France has published three books with Bloodaxe, the anthology *Sixty Women Poets* (1993) and her collections *Red* (1992) and *The Gentleness of the Very Tall* (1994), a Poetry Book Society Recommendation. She has worked on several collaborations with artists and public art commissions. She was awarded the Arts Foundation's first Poetry Fellowship in 1993, and lives in Northumberland.

Charlie Hardwick was born in Wallsend. A former DSS clerk who stumbled into acting, she has performed with the Virgins since their conception. She has worked extensively with Living Memory, Northern Stage Company and Live Theatre on plays including *Andorra, Your Home in the West, Buffalo Girls* and *Close the Coalhouse Door*. She appeared in *Little Richard Wrecked My Marriage* (My Aunt Fanny Films and Channel Four), *Break My Bones* and *I Luv Jimmy Spud* (Radio 4), and was Duncan's Mam in *Byker Grove*.

Kay Hepplewhite is an original Virgin. She worked as an actor for several years with companies including NE1 Theatre, Belgrade Theatre, Coventry, and Living Memory. She is now a lecturer in performing arts.

Maria Jastrzebska moved to London from Poland as a small child. She now lives in Brighton, where she teaches women's self-defence. She claims Anna Swir as 'a heroine and inspiration'.

Fiona MacPherson moved to Newcastle in 1979. A television and theatre actor, and a mother of two, she is an experienced Virgin. A founder member of NE1 Theatre Company, she sang with Red Music, and has worked with Northern Stage and Northumberland Theatre Company. She was a singer with A Better Thing, a group of poets and musicians, and with Living Memory Trio. Her TV work includes *Little Richard Wrecked My Marriage* (My Aunt Fanny Films and Channel Four), *Harry* (BBC 1) and Catherine Cookson's *The Glass Virgin* (Tyne Tees).

Elma Mitchell was born 1919 in Airdrie, and now lives in Somerset. She worked as a librarian, and in broadcasting, publishing and journalism. She has had four books of poetry published by Peterloo Poets: *People Etcetera: Poems New & Selected* (1987) includes work from two earlier collections, *The Poor Man in the Flesh* (1976) and *The Human Cage* (1979); a subsequent book, *Furnished Rooms* (1983), is out of print.

Ellen Phethean was born in 1952. She has had her poetry broadcast on *Loose Ends* and *Poetry Please* (Radio 4), and performs as a poet in her own right. She has written and performed with The Poetry Virgins for several years. She has two sons and is a creative writing tutor.

June P. Portlock is a founder member of Future Tense, a poetry performing poetry group based in Gateshead, where she works as a tutor in creative writing for the housebound. She won the Vane Tempest Poetry Prize in 1993, and was a finalist in the Sid Chaplin Short Story Competition in 1994 and in the One Voice Monologue Competition in 1993.

Anna Swir was a distinguished Polish poet. Born in 1909, she was a nurse in the Second World War, and died in 1984. A collection of her poems, *Fat Like the Sun*, was published by the Women's Press in 1986.

BOOKINGS: The Poetry Virgins, c/o Diamond Twig Press, 5 Bentinck Road, Newcastle upon Tyne NE4 6UT.